JAMESTOWN EDUCAT

In the Spotlight™

Volume 2

Levels B–D

Henry Billings

Melissa Billings

Glencoe

New York, New York   Columbus, Ohio   Chicago, Illinois   Peoria, Illinois   Woodland Hills, California

JAMESTOWN 🚢 EDUCATION

The McGraw·Hill Companies

Copyright © 2007 The McGraw-Hill Companies, Inc.
All rights reserved. Except as permitted under the United States
Copyright Act, no part of this publication may be reproduced or
distributed in any form or by any means, or stored in a database or
retrieval system, without prior written permission of the publisher.

ISBN-13: 978-0-07-874322-1
ISBN-10: 0-07-874322-2

Send all queries to:
Glencoe/McGraw-Hill
8787 Orion Place
Columbus, OH 43240-4027

2 3 4 5 6 7 8 9 10 021 10 09 08 07

Contents

Unit Three

To the Student

This book has nine articles about celebrities, or famous people, in the world today. Some of the celebrities are movie or television stars. Some are sports players. Others are authors or musicians.

The lives of these stars can inspire us. Some of the stars had tough times while growing up. They worked very hard to find success. Others had to stay focused on their dreams even when other people thought they would fail. And some had to get through challenges even after they became well-known.

In this book you will work on these three specific reading skills:

Using Context

Cause and Effect

Making Predictions

You will also work on other reading and vocabulary skills. This will help you understand and think about what you read. The lessons include types of questions often found on state and national tests. Completing the questions can help you get ready for tests you may have to take later.

How to Use This Book

About the Book

This book has three units. Each unit has three lessons. Each lesson has an article about a celebrity followed by practice exercises.

Working Through Each Lesson

Photo Start each lesson by looking at the photo. Read the title and subtitle to get an idea of what the article will focus on.

Think About What You Know, Word Power, Reading Skill This page will help you prepare to read.

Article Now read about the celebrity. Enjoy!

Activities Complete all the activities. Then check your work. Your teacher will give you an answer key to do this. Record the number of your correct answers for each activity. At the end of the lesson, add up your total score for parts A, B, and C. Then find your percentage score in the table. Record your percentage score on the Comprehension and Critical Thinking Progress Graph on page 105.

Compare and Contrast Chart At the end of each unit, you will complete a Compare and Contrast Chart. The chart will help you see what some of the celebrities in the unit have in common.

My Personal Dictionary In the back of this book, you can jot down words you would like to know more about. Later you can ask your teacher or a classmate what the words mean. Then you can add the definitions in your own words.

Lang Lang

Shania Twain

Deion Branch

Lang Lang
Piano Man

Birth Name Lang Lang
Birth Date and Place June 14, 1982; Shenyang, China
Home Philadelphia, Pennsylvania

Think About What You Know

Have you ever taken music lessons? Would you like to know how to play the piano? Read the article and find out about Lang Lang and his music.

Word Power

What do the words below tell you about the article?

pianist a person who plays the piano

reaction something that a person does or feels because of something that has happened

classical a kind of music that began in the 1700s, such as music written by Mozart

accent the way people say words that shows where they are from

passion a strong liking for something

Reading Skill

Using Context Context clues can help you find the meaning of a word that you don't understand. Context clues are other words in the same sentence or in nearby sentences. If you don't understand a word, look for clues around it that might help you. Then try to find the meaning.

Example	
New Word	She has always enjoyed singing with a group. That's
Context Clues	why she sings in a chorus.

If you don't know the meaning of the word *chorus*, you can use the clues "singing with a group," and "she sings in" to help you find the meaning. From these clues, what do you think *chorus* means?

3

Lang Lang

Piano Man

Can a baby enjoy and understand music? Some people may say no. But then how do you explain the Chinese **pianist** Lang Lang?

2   Lang Lang was born in 1982 in northern China. From the beginning, his parents could see that he loved music. Says his father, "Even at one month old, our son had a special **reaction** to music."

3   When Lang Lang was two years old, he was watching TV. A cartoon came on. The cartoon showed a mouse playing the piano. The mouse was playing a famous piano piece by Franz Liszt. Lang Lang listened to this **classical** music. Then he walked over to his family's piano and began to play. He didn't just bang on the keys. He played the exact notes he had heard on the cartoon. Lang Lang's parents could see that their son was gifted.

4   When Lang Lang was three years old, his parents found him a piano teacher. After just two years, Lang Lang could play many hard pieces. He did not sit down when he played. He would not have been able to reach the pedals. Instead he stood up. Even so, he had to stretch his arms wide to reach all the keys.

5   At age five, Lang Lang gave his first show. He was not at all nervous. To him, it was fun. "I remember I was just so excited to go out and play," he says.

6   By the time Lang Lang was nine, he needed more training than he could get in his hometown of Shenyang. He needed to go to Beijing. That is the capital of China. But going there meant breaking up the family. Lang Lang's mother worked as a telephone engineer in Shenyang. The family needed the money she earned. They could not afford to have her leave her job. So she stayed in Shenyang while Lang Lang's father moved with him to Beijing, an 11-hour train ride away.

7   Life in Beijing was not easy for Lang Lang. He and his father lived in a tiny apartment with no heat. Lang Lang was cold all the time. "Sometimes my father would go to bed before me and warm up the sheets for when I went to sleep," Lang Lang says. Every morning at 5:00 A.M., Lang Lang got up to practice the piano. Then he went to school. When he came home, he practiced more. "I practiced piano five hours a day!" he notes.

8   Lang Lang missed his mother terribly. He also had trouble making friends at school. He had a heavy northern **accent.** Speaking differently than the other kids made him feel like an outsider. He didn't feel like he belonged there. And worst of all, he did not get along with his new music teacher. "I had a teacher who didn't like me," he says. He tried to please her. But everything he did seemed wrong. For the first time ever, he did not have fun playing the piano. It made him sad. At last, he says, the teacher "kicked me out of her class."

Skill Break

Using Context

Look at paragraph 6 on this page. Find the word *afford* in the middle of the paragraph. What **clues** in the paragraph can help you find the meaning of *afford*?

From the clues, what do you think *afford* means?

9   Lang Lang was very upset. But when he found a new music teacher, things got better. "I got a good teacher, and everything just changed," he says. Once again he began to enjoy making music. His spirits rose, and he started to make friends at school. Soon he felt happy again.

10   Over the next few years, Lang Lang's talent grew. He continued to play the piano many hours a day. He played with great energy, putting his whole body into the music. He pounded the keys so often and so hard that many of the strings broke. "In the end, some 30 tones didn't work," he says. "I must have broken about 70 strings. I didn't mind. I just kept playing, and I replaced the missing notes inside my head."

11   By 1997 Lang Lang felt ready to do more. He and his father moved to Philadelphia. There Lang Lang studied at the Curtis Institute. The teachers there helped him play even better.

12   His big chance came when he was 17. He tried out for Chicago's Ravinia Festival. This is the oldest summer music festival in the United States. Many famous people play there every year. Lang Lang knew his try-out went well. "I was supposed to play for 20 minutes," he says. "But I played for two hours." Still, he thought it would be a couple of years before he got to play at Ravinia. He was surprised when the phone rang the very next morning. A Ravinia pianist had gotten sick. Would Lang Lang like to fill in for him?

Fun Facts

- *Lang Lang* means "smart man with open mind."
- He likes playing table tennis and table soccer.
- He plays piano in 150 shows a year.
- After playing he soaks his hands in hot water and rubs them.

Lang Lang plays on an outdoor stage in Hong Kong. He often does shows to raise money for children who are in need.

13   Twelve hours later, Lang Lang took the stage. He amazed everyone. In that one night, he became famous. One Chicago paper called him the "biggest, most exciting keyboard talent" to come along in years.

14   Since then, many people have become fans of Lang Lang. People around the world love his style. They love to watch his hands and hair fly in all directions. They love his big grin. Most of all, they love the **passion** he brings to his music. Many say he is the greatest pianist of our times.

15   It's not just classical music fans who know about Lang Lang. He has reached out beyond that group. His music was used on the TV show *Joan of Arcadia*. He has also been on *The Tonight Show*.

16   Lang Lang sees that the world is full of many kinds of music. It flows from people's hearts and minds, he says. So of course music comes in different forms. He loves classical music. But he also likes Britney Spears, Eminem, and Michael Jackson. For him, all forms of music have one thing in common. "We should always remember," he says, "that music is for sharing."

A   Understanding What You Read

◆ **Fill in the circle next to the correct answer.**

1. What first caused Lang Lang's parents to think he should have piano lessons?

   ○ A. He practiced more than five hours a day.

   ○ B. He could play music he had heard on TV.

   ○ C. He did not sit down when he played.

2. When Lang Lang moved to Beijing, his

   ○ A. mother got a new job fixing telephones.

   ○ B. father went on a trip to Philadelphia.

   ○ C. music teacher didn't like him.

3. Lang Lang got his first big chance in the United States when

   ○ A. a Ravinia Festival pianist got sick.

   ○ B. he played piano on *The Tonight Show*.

   ○ C. a Chicago newspaper wrote about him.

4. The author probably wrote this article in order to

   ○ A. teach the reader about life in China.

   ○ B. tell the reader about a great pianist.

   ○ C. make the reader want piano lessons.

5. Which sentence **best** states the main idea of the article?

   ○ A. Lang Lang is famous for being a great piano player.

   ○ B. Lang Lang's music is well-known around the world.

   ○ C. Lang Lang started piano lessons when he was three years old.

_____ Number of Correct Answers: Part A

B Using Context

◆ Read the paragraph below. Look for context clues that tell you what the word *gifted* means. Underline the context clues in the paragraph. Then fill in the circle next to the correct meaning of *gifted*.

1.

When Lang Lang was two years old, he was watching TV. A cartoon came on. The cartoon showed a mouse playing the piano. The mouse was playing a famous piano piece by Franz Liszt. Lang Lang listened to this classical music. Then he walked over to his family's piano and began to play. He didn't just bang on the keys. He played the exact notes he had heard on the cartoon. Lang Lang's parents could see that their son was <u>gifted</u>.

○ A. getting many presents
○ B. very good at something
○ C. funny looking

◆ Reread paragraph 8 in the article. Find the word *outsider* in the middle of the paragraph. Look for a clue about the meaning of *outsider*. Write the clue below. Then write what you think *outsider* means.

2. Context Clue: _____

Outsider means: _____

_____

┌───┐
│ _____ Number of Correct Answers: Part B │
└───┘

C Using Words

Complete each sentence with a word from the box. Write the missing word on the line.

pianist	classical	passion
reaction	accent	

1. My brother has a _____ for collecting rocks.

2. The teacher asked the _____ to play a song for

the class.

3. The new boy spoke with an _____.

4. Her _____ to the joke was to laugh.

5. My mom's favorite music is _____.

Choose one of the words from the box. Write a new sentence using the word.

6. word: _____

_____

_____

_____ Number of Correct Answers: Part C

D Writing About It

Write a Story

◆ What happened when Lang Lang tried out for Chicago's Ravinia Festival? Write a story about it. Finish the sentences below to write your story. Use the checklist on page 103 to check your work.

In 1999 Lang Lang tried out for Chicago's Ravinia Festival. The

Ravina Festival is _____.

During Lang Lang's tryout, they let him play _____

_____.

The phone rang the next morning and Lang Lang found out _____

_____

_____.

When Lang Lang played at the show, people thought _____

_____.

Lesson 1 Add your correct answers from parts A, B, and C to get your total score. Then find the percentage for your total score on the chart below. Record your percentage on the graph on page 105.

_____ Total Score for Parts A, B, and C

_____ Percentage

Total Score	1	2	3	4	5	6	7	8	9	10	11	12	13
Percentage	8	15	23	31	38	46	54	62	69	77	85	92	100

Shania Twain

A Happy Ending

Birth Name Eilleen Regina Edwards
Birth Date and Place August 28, 1965; Windsor, Ontario, Canada
Home Tour-de-Peilz, Switzerland

Think About What You Know

Have you ever had to go without something you needed? What did that feel like? Read the article and find out about Shania Twain and how she made it through hard times.

Word Power

What do the words below tell you about the article?

suffer to feel pain or go through hard times

condiments something eaten with food to make the food taste better

petrified not able to move because of fear

pressure a heavy feeling caused by worry

content not wanting anything more than what you already have

Reading Skill

Cause and Effect Many stories and articles show cause and effect. A **cause** tells *why* something happened. An **effect** tells *what* happened. The cause happens first. Then the effect happens. The word *because* can help you find the cause. The word *so* can help you find the effect.

Example	
Cause	My cousin wants to save money to buy a car. Today
Effect	he started looking for a job.

The cause in this paragraph is "My cousin wants to save money to buy a car." The effect is "he started looking for a job." To find the cause, you can ask yourself *why.* When you answer the question *why,* the words that come after the word *because* show the cause. *Why* did the cousin start looking for a job?

Shania Twain

A Happy Ending

Shania Twain knows what it's like to be poor. She knows what it's like to be *very* poor. Today Twain is a superstar who has millions of dollars. But her early life was filled with hard times. That may be why she has put so much effort into her career. "I would do anything I had to," she says, "to make sure I never had to **suffer** again."

2   Twain grew up in a small town in northern Canada. She was one of five children raised by Sharon and Jerry Twain. Jerry was Shania's stepfather, but she thinks of him as her true father. Jerry was a member of the First Nation tribe called the Ojibwa. Through him, Shania also became a member of this Native American tribe. "My dad's side of the family was the side we grew up with," says Twain. "So it was the Indians that were really our family."

3   Jerry worked when he could, but jobs were not easy to find. Often the family had no money coming in. "Our electricity would sometimes get shut off," says Twain. The heat would get shut off too. With no money for the laundry, Twain had to wash her clothes in the bathtub.

4   To get food, Jerry hunted for moose. Twain sometimes went with him. She also helped him trap rabbits. Still, she says, "There were a lot of times we didn't have food." Twain remembers thinking that anyone with enough money to buy a roast beef sandwich must be really rich. Her family often didn't even have enough money for peanut butter. Twain made sandwiches out of nothing but bread and **condiments** such as mustard and mayonnaise.

5   Money was not Twain's only problem. She was a shy girl. She had a beautiful voice, and she loved to sing, but she didn't like to perform in front of others. She spent hours in her room making up songs and singing them to herself. Her parents noticed this. They didn't care that she was shy. They thought she had enough talent to become a singer, and they were eager to see it happen.

6   To get her started, her parents began taking Twain to bars to perform. Because she was just eight years old, she could not be present when alcohol was served. So Twain's parents would wait until after the last drink had been poured. Then, around 1:00 A.M., they would wake Twain up. They would get her out of bed and take her to bars to sing.

7   "The bars were rough," Twain says. "They were smoky, everyone was half-drunk, and fights would often break out. A lot of the time I was half-asleep because I'd work late nights but still have to get up for school the next morning."

8   Twain's parents also took her to talent shows. For Twain, these were even worse. "I was so **petrified.** I used to get sick," she says. "I was shy, nervous, didn't like the **pressure.**" Twain knew her parents wanted her to become a star. But as she puts it, that was "their dream. I dreamed of being a kid."

Skill Break
Cause and Effect
Look at paragraph 7 on this page. This paragraph shows cause and effect.

The **effect** is that Twain was half-asleep a lot of the time. What is the **cause?**

What **question** did you ask to help you find the cause?

9 In a way, all of this did help Twain. It got her used to performing. She also learned that people liked her voice. So when she was 16, she joined a band. After high school, she continued singing. She moved to Toronto. During the day, she worked as a secretary. At night she sang in clubs.

10 Twain may have hoped the hard times had passed. But when she was 22, a very sad thing happened. Her parents were killed in a car accident. That left Twain's little brothers and sister all alone. Twain knew what she had to do. As their big sister, she had always looked out for them. Now she would have to be their parent. "I didn't have a choice," she says. "My brothers were 13 and 14, and my sister had just turned 18, but had still been living with my parents and wasn't ready to go off into the world, so it was up to me."

11 Twain moved them into a small house in Huntsville, Ontario. She got a singing job there. Once again, life was hard. There was just enough money to get by. When the well they used for water went dry, Twain had to wash the family's clothes in a river. "I felt totally lost," she says. "It was like being thrown into the deep end of a pool and just having to swim." For three years, she struggled like this. Finally her brothers and sister were ready to move out and live on their own. That meant Twain could at last begin to live her own life.

Fun Facts

- Twain's family calls her Leenie.
- She does not drink, smoke, or eat meat.
- She likes to work in the garden.
- She loves riding horses.

Shania Twain is not shy about singing on stage anymore.

12   Over the next few years, Twain worked hard on her music career. She went to Nashville. There she made several hit records. In fact, *Come On Over* became the most successful record ever made by a woman. Twain also fell in love. In 1993 she married record producer Robert John "Mutt" Lange. They had a son, Eja, in 2001.

13   Today Shania Twain has a good life. She has love, money, and a great career. She is glad that her career has gone so well. Even so, she says, "I don't . . . need to be a star my whole life to be **content.** I didn't have to become rich and famous to have a happy ending. I have enough food and a house. That's success."

◆ **Fill in the circle next to the correct answer.**

1. Choose the statement below that shows someone's opinion.

○ A. Her parents thought she had enough talent to be a singer.

○ B. Her brothers and sisters moved out on their own.

○ C. She married record producer Robert John "Mutt" Lange.

2. When Twain was growing up, she helped her father

○ A. look for a job.

○ B. wash the clothes.

○ C. hunt for moose.

3. In which paragraph did you find your answer to question 2?

○ A. paragraph 4

○ B. paragraph 5

○ C. paragraph 6

4. When Twain went to Nashville, she

○ A. lived with her brothers and sisters.

○ B. made several hit records.

○ C. worked as a secretary.

5. Twain's life as a child and Twain's life now are different because Twain

○ A. couldn't sing as a child, but now she sings very well.

○ B. was lonely as a child, but now she has friends.

○ C. didn't have enough food as a child, but now she does.

_____ Number of Correct Answers: Part A

B Understanding Cause and Effect

◆ Read the paragraph below. The paragraph shows cause and effect. The effect is that Twain spent hours alone in her room singing. Fill in the circle next to the sentence that shows the **cause**.

1.

   Money was not Twain's only problem. She was a shy girl. She had a beautiful voice, and she loved to sing, but she didn't like to perform in front of others. She spent hours in her room making up songs and singing them to herself. Her parents noticed this. They didn't care that she was shy. They thought she had enough talent to become a singer, and they were eager to see it happen.

   ○ A. She loved to sing, but not in front of others.
   ○ B. She had a beautiful voice, but not enough talent.
   ○ C. She made up her own songs, but didn't tell her parents.

◆ Reread paragraph 11 in the article. The paragraph shows cause and effect. The effect is that Twain had to wash the family's clothes in the river. What question can you ask to find the **cause?** Write the question and the cause on the lines below.

2. Question: _____

_____

Cause: _____

_____

_____ Number of Correct Answers: Part B

C Using Words

Complete each sentence with a word from the box. Write the missing word on the line.

suffer	petrified	content
condiments	pressure	

1. After eating a nice meal, she felt _____.

2. He was _____ by the sound of the lion's roar.

3. Mustard is one of my favorite _____.

4. The man's sore back caused him to _____.

5. The students felt a lot of _____ to do well in the spelling bee.

Choose one of the words from the box. Write a new sentence using the word.

6. word: _____

_____

_____

_____ Number of Correct Answers: Part C

D Writing About It

Write Your Thoughts

◆ Answer the question below. Use the checklist on page 103 to check your work.

What was most surprising or interesting to you about this article?

_____

_____

How Did You Do?

◆ Finish the sentence below. Use the checklist on page 103 to check your work.

Before reading the article, I already knew _____

_____

_____.

Lesson 2 Add your correct answers from parts A, B, and C to get your total score. Then find the percentage for your total score on the chart below. Record your percentage on the graph on page 105.

_____ Total Score for Parts A, B, and C

_____ Percentage

Total Score	1	2	3	4	5	6	7	8	9	10	11	12	13
Percentage	8	15	23	31	38	46	54	62	69	77	85	92	100

Deion Branch

Learning a Good Lesson

Birth Name Anthony Deion Branch Jr.

Birth Date and Place July 18, 1979; Albany, Georgia

Home near Boston, Massachusetts

Think About What You Know

Have you ever had a second chance to get something right? What was it like to start over again? Read the article and find out about Deion Branch's second chance.

Word Power

What do the words below tell you about the article?

bleak not good or without hope

attitude a way of thinking, acting, or feeling about something

humble not thinking or acting like you are more important than others

wide receiver a football player who lines up at the end of a row of players and runs to catch the ball

glory the special attention that people give to someone who they think is great

Reading Skill

Making Predictions A **prediction** is a good guess about what will happen later in a story or an article. Good readers make predictions based on clues from the text and what they already know. Good readers change their predictions as they read more of the story or article.

> **Example**

They packed the car with large towels, sunblock, cold drinks, and a picnic basket. Then the whole family got in the car.

From the information in the paragraph, you can predict that *the family will go somewhere.* The clue to make this prediction is "the whole family got in the car." You might also predict that *the family will go to the beach.* What clues tell you that the family might go to the beach? How does what you already know help you use these clues?

Deion Branch

Learning a Good Lesson

In 1996 life was good for Deion Branch. He was a star football player at Monroe High School in Albany, Georgia. He played so well that he was offered a full scholarship at the University of Florida. But then Branch made some poor choices. By the time he finished high school, he had lost the scholarship. The University of Florida no longer wanted him. His bright future suddenly looked **bleak.**

2   Branch knew it was his own fault. His **attitude** had been bad. He had thought he was too cool for school. As he says, "I got a big head. I started hanging with my friends and stopped going to class." His grades went down quickly. The people at the University of Florida changed their minds about him. They decided he was not right for their program.

3   It was a tough lesson. Branch might have become angry or bitter. But he didn't. Instead he thought carefully about what he had done. He took responsibility for what had happened. He even says, "I'm glad that happened to me early. It taught me not to take things for granted."

4   Branch decided to change. Never again would he act like nothing could go wrong. He would work hard and stay **humble.** With this new attitude, he hoped he might still have a football career. After all, he had surprised people before.

5   Back in middle school, he had been told he was too small to play football. The coach had not even let him try out. Branch had stayed with the game anyway. He had gone on to be a great **wide receiver** in high school. So when he lost his spot at the University of Florida, he knew what he had to do. He had to start from the beginning. He had to prove himself all over again.

6   Branch signed up for Jones County Junior College in Ellisville, Mississippi. There he worked hard in his classes and on the football field. He did very well. After two years, he won a spot at the University of Louisville. This school was harder. Branch struggled with his classes. But this time he kept working. The first year his grades were so poor he could not play sports at all. By the second year, he was doing better. He was able to return to football.

7   During his first football season at Louisville, Branch caught passes for more than 1,000 yards. The next year he did the same thing. He also became a team captain. The high-school kid with the bad attitude had become a lovable college player.

8   In 2002 Branch turned professional. He hoped a National Football League team would draft him. The San Francisco 49ers thought about it. But they decided he was too small. It's easy to see why. Deion Branch stands only 5 feet 9 inches tall. He weighs less than 200 pounds. Most professional football players are much, much bigger. Even receivers like Branch are usually at least 6 feet tall.

Skill Break
Making Predictions

Look at paragraph 8 on this page. This paragraph tells about what happened when Branch turned professional. Using clues in the paragraph, what do you think is most likely to **happen next?**

What **clues** did you use to make your prediction?

How does **what you already know** help you use the clues?

As you read the next page, check to see if what happens next matches your prediction.

9 Luckily, the New England Patriots saw things a different way. They didn't think Branch's small size was a problem. They made him their second-round draft pick.

10 From the beginning, the Patriots liked Branch. They thought he was a good player. More than that, they liked his attitude.

11 "He doesn't have the height, but he has the heart," says teammate Fred Baxter. "Deion plays like he's 6 foot 4 or 6 foot 5."

12 "He's really a pleasure to work with," says head coach Bill Belichick. "Deion has been . . . one of our best team players since he's been up here."

13 During his first two years with the Patriots, Branch made some great plays. His best game came in the 2004 Super Bowl. There he caught 10 passes for 143 yards. Still, Branch remained a quiet member of the team. He didn't seek **glory.** He was happy just to be on the team.

14 The next season, the Patriots again returned to the Super Bowl. Branch had been out much of the year with a knee problem, but he was back in time for this game. And he was given a key spot in the lineup.

15 As he prepared for the big day, Branch thought about how far he had come. He thought about all the people who had helped him along the way. And he decided there was one thing he had to do. He had to call up all his old coaches to say thanks.

Fun Facts

- Branch is the father of twin boys.
- In high school, he played football and soccer and ran track.
- He likes to listen to R&B and rap music.
- He collects old cars.

Deion Branch looks for space to run after catching a pass.

16   On the day of the 2005 Super Bowl, Branch did just that. He called all 13 of his old coaches, starting with the ones who had coached him as a child. It took two hours. "I was crying half the time," he says. "It's hard, but I don't want them to think I've left them behind. I want them to know I'm thinking about them all the time."

17   That day Branch played a terrific game. He caught 11 passes for 133 yards. Only two other receivers had ever caught that many passes in a Super Bowl game. When the game ended, Branch was named Most Valuable Player.

18   It was a big moment for him, but he didn't forget the lesson he had learned back in high school. He stayed humble. He thanked his coaches for the chance to play. He also thanked his teammates for doing so well.

19   Deion Branch had become a winner both on the field and off. He was a star player. He was also someone who understood that there is more to life than football. As he says, "I don't want people to look at me as . . . just a football player. I want people to look at me as a good person."

A Understanding What You Read

◆ Fill in the circle next to the correct answer.

1. Branch was a quiet player on the Patriots team because he
   ○ A. had a lot of problems with his knee.
   ○ B. was smaller than the other players.
   ○ C. was just happy to be on the team.

2. Right before the 2005 Super Bowl, Branch cried when he
   ○ A. thought the Patriots might lose the game.
   ○ B. called his old coaches to thank them.
   ○ C. found out he would not be able to play.

3. From what you read in the article, which of these is probably true?
   ○ A. The 49ers won the Super Bowl in 2002.
   ○ B. The 49ers didn't need any new players in 2002.
   ○ C. The 49ers wish they had drafted Branch in 2002.

4. If you were a high school football coach, how would you use the information in the article to help your team?
   ○ A. I would give them all college scholarships.
   ○ B. I would make sure they watch the Super Bowl.
   ○ C. I would warn them against letting their grades fall.

5. Which of the following groups would this article fit into?
   ○ A. Winners On and Off the Field
   ○ B. Best Football Games Ever Played
   ○ C. How to Get a College Scholarship

_____ Number of Correct Answers: Part A

B Making Predictions

◆ Read the paragraph below. Look at the clues in the paragraph. Fill in the circle next to the prediction that is **most likely** to happen based on the clues.

1.

Back in middle school, he had been told he was too small to play football. The coach had not even let him try out. Branch had stayed with the game anyway. He had gone on to be a great wide receiver in high school. So when he lost his spot at the University of Florida, he knew what he had to do. He had to start from the beginning. He had to prove himself all over again.

○ A. Branch will move to Florida and get a job.
○ B. Branch will decide that his middle-school coach was right.
○ C. Branch will work hard and prove he can play college football.

◆ What clues in the paragraph above helped you make the prediction? How did what you already know help you make the prediction? Write the clues and what you already know on the lines.

2. Clues: _____

_____

_____

What I Know: _____

_____

_____ Number of Correct Answers: Part B

C Using Words

◆ Complete each sentence with a word or words from the box. Write the missing word on the line.

bleak	humble	glory
attitude	wide receiver	

1. No one knew he was a great cook because he was very

_____.

2. He was the best _____ on the football team.

3. She enjoyed the _____ that came with winning first place.

4. Teachers like her because she has a good _____.

5. Since their two best players were gone, the team's chances of

winning were _____.

◆ Choose one of the words from the box. Write a new sentence using the word.

6. word: _____

_____

_____ Number of Correct Answers: Part C

D Writing About It

Write a Postcard

◆ Write a postcard to Deion Branch. Finish the sentences below to write your postcard. Use the checklist on page 103 to check your work.

Dear Mr. Branch,

I just read an article about you. I think you _____

_____

_____.

I liked it when _____

_____.

If I were you, _____

_____.

Sincerely,

_____

Mr. Deion Branch
123 Branch Ave.
Deionsville, USA

Lesson 3 Add your correct answers from parts A, B, and C to get your total score. Then find the percentage for your total score on the chart below. Record your percentage on the graph on page 105.

_____ Total Score for Parts A, B, and C

_____ Percentage

Total Score	1	2	3	4	5	6	7	8	9	10	11	12	13
Percentage	8	15	23	31	38	46	54	62	69	77	85	92	100

Compare and Contrast

◆ Think about the celebrities, or famous people, in Unit One. Pick two articles that tell about celebrities who made a change for the better. Use information from the articles to fill in this chart.

Celebrity's Name		
What did the celebrity change?		
Why did the celebrity make the change?		
How did the change make things better?		

Michelle Wie

Johnny Depp

Tim McGraw

Michelle Wie

Young Golf Star

Birth Name Michelle Sung Wie

Birth Date and Place October 11, 1989; Honolulu, Hawaii

Home Honolulu, Hawaii

Think About What You Know

Can you think of any sports where kids do as well or better than adults? Do you know any kids who are really good at golf? Read the article and find out about young golfer Michelle Wie.

Word Power

What do the words below tell you about the article?

tournament a group of contests or games

professional doing something in order to earn money and make a living

amateur a person who does something for fun, not to earn money

qualify to be considered good enough

par in golf, a set number of strokes a good player would take to finish a hole or a course

Reading Skill

Using Context Context clues can help you find the meaning of a word that you don't understand. Context clues are other words in the same sentence or in nearby sentences. If you don't understand a word, look for clues around it that might help you. Then try to find the meaning.

> ### Example
>
> **Context Clues**
>
> **New Word**
>
> Yesterday I could not find my golf clubs. I knew they were somewhere in the garage. The garage was full of tools, boxes, and junk. It took a long time to look through all the clutter. Finally I found my golf clubs in the corner.

If you don't know the meaning of the word *clutter,* you can use the context clues "full of tools, boxes, and junk" and "it took a long time to look through" to help you find the meaning. From these clues, what do you think *clutter* means?

Michelle Wie

Young Golf Star

She was through. After two rounds of golf, Michelle Wie was out of the **tournament.** Her score was not good enough for her to move on to the final rounds. But Wie wasn't upset. "I'm not disappointed," she said. "I'm just happy to be here."

2   Wie really meant what she said. For her, just playing at this event was an honor. After all, this was a major tournament. It was an important event given by a group called the Ladies' Professional Golf Association (LPGA). That meant it was for women who were **professional** golfers. Yet Wie was not a professional. She was an **amateur.** And on top of that, she was just 12 years old.

3   Wie was the youngest player ever to **qualify** for the tournament. She was the youngest player ever to qualify for *any* LPGA tour event. So she had reason to be happy. It didn't matter that she hadn't won. She knew there would be plenty of winning moments in her future.

4   The very next year Wie did win. She won a national tournament for amateurs. This was a big deal. People from all over the country came to compete against each other. It was called the U. S. Women's Amateur Public Links Championship. Wie became the youngest person ever to win it. "I've never won a national title," she said, "I'm happy out of my mind."

5   Michelle Wie was born with lots of golf talent. She has worked hard to make the most of it. She began playing golf when she was just four years old. Her father took her to the golf driving range with him. To his surprise, she hit the ball so hard she almost fell over. "Sometimes it would go right, sometimes left, but it didn't matter," says her father. "She just wanted to hit it hard."

6   Soon Wie started practicing in the family's back yard in Honolulu, Hawaii. By age five, she could hit the ball more than 100 yards. She was in danger of hitting neighbors' houses and cars. So she had to refrain from playing at home. She stopped practicing in the backyard, and her parents began taking her to real golf courses. At first, other golfers grumbled when they saw a five-year-old walking onto the course. They were sure she would hold them up by making lots of terrible shots. Instead, she proved to be as good as they were, or better.

7   For a while, Wie's parents could still beat her. Her mother, Bo, had been the 1985 female amateur golf champion of Korea. Her father, BJ, was also a fine golfer. But by the time Wie was eight she could beat them both. The following year they gave up playing with her. She was simply too good for them. Wie was so accomplished, in fact, that many people believe she was a better player at her age than Tiger Woods had been.

8   Wie knew a lot about Tiger Woods. He was her role model. She knew that Woods played in the Professional Golf Association (PGA), where the men play. She wanted to play in the PGA just like him. Only a few women had ever qualified for a PGA tournament.

9   Wie soon got her chance. In 2004 she entered her first PGA event. Wie was only 14 at the time. That made her two years younger than Woods had been in his first PGA outing.

Skill Break

Using Context

Look at paragraph 4 on page 36. Find the word *compete* in the middle of the paragraph.

What **clues** in the paragraph can help you find the meaning of *compete*?

From the clues, what do you think *compete* means?

10　　During the first two days of the tournament, Wie shot even **par.** She impressed everyone. Even the professional golfers thought she played well. She was just a ninth grader, but she was very strong. She stood six feet tall. She had a beautiful swing and made great drives. She hit the ball off the tee farther than many of the men.

11　　"It's pretty incredible," said PGA golfer Jerry Kelly.

12　　"She can play on this tour . . . there's no reason why she shouldn't be out here," agreed PGA golfer Ernie Els.

13　　Wie didn't win the event. In fact, she missed the cut by one stroke. Only about half the golfers make the cut. Those who do get to play the final two rounds. The others have to go home. Although Wie didn't make it, she still beat or tied 64 golfers. These were not just any golfers. They were among the best golfers in the world.

14　　Wie was upset to be so close and yet miss the cut. "Just one more shot, and I would have made it," she said. "It's killing me now."

15　　Wie returned to Honolulu. She had to go back to high school. She also wanted to work more on her golf game. As her first coach, Casey Nakama, says, "She just works really hard."

Fun Facts

▸ Wie speaks both English and Korean.
▸ Her favorite class in school is math.

▸ She believes that seeing red ladybugs on the golf course is a sign of good luck.

Michelle Wie watches her shot during an LPGA Tour event.

16   Wie is also a fast learner. Nakama remembers when he taught her how to hit the ball out of the sand. He showed her the right swing a few times. Then Wie grabbed her club and jumped into the sand. Learning to hit out of the sand is difficult for most people, but not for Wie. Says Nakama, "By the fourth shot she was hitting it just right, copying it perfectly. I was thinking, 'Wow, this is not normal.'"

17   Normal or not, Michelle Wie is serious about golf. She turned professional on October 5, 2005. Six days later she had her 16th birthday. She even hopes to win the PGA Masters' Tournament some day. This is one of the biggest tournaments in all of golf. Tiger Woods has won it more than once. Wie wants to do the same. She should have a lot of chances. After all, she plans to be playing golf for many years to come.

A Understanding What You Read

◆ Fill in the circle next to the correct answer.

1. At her first LPGA event, Wie was the

- ○ A. best player.
- ○ B. first female player.
- ○ C. youngest player.

2. What caused Wie's parents to take her to a real golf course when she was five years old?

- ○ A. She wanted to be like Tiger Woods.
- ○ B. She could hit the ball more than 100 yards.
- ○ C. She wanted to go golfing with her mother.

3. Michelle Wie and Tiger Woods are alike because both

- ○ A. played in the PGA when they were very young.
- ○ B. won the first PGA tour they ever entered.
- ○ C. have parents who were professional golfers.

4. Wie was upset after her first PGA tournament because

- ○ A. she didn't want to go back to Hawaii.
- ○ B. the other golfers did not welcome her.
- ○ C. she missed being in the finals by one shot.

5. Which sentence **best** states the lesson about life that this article teaches?

- ○ A. It's never too late to learn something new.
- ○ B. Winning is more important than hard work.
- ○ C. Young people are able to do amazing things.

_____ Number of Correct Answers: Part A

B Using Context

◆ Read the paragraph below. Look for context clues that tell you what the word *association* means. Underline the context clues in the paragraph. Then fill in the circle next to the correct meaning of *association*.

1.

Wie really meant what she said. For her, just playing at this event was an honor. After all, this was a major tournament. It was an important event given by a group called the Ladies' Professional Golf <u>Association</u> (LPGA). That meant it was for women who were professional golfers. Yet Wie was not a professional. She was an amateur. And on top of that, she was just 12 years old.

○ A. a magazine that prints information about sports
○ B. a group of people with common interests
○ C. a business that makes and sells equipment

◆ Read paragraph 10 in the article. Find the word *impressed* in the second sentence. Look for context clues about the meaning of the word *impressed*. Write the clues on the lines below. Then write what you think *impressed* means.

2. Context Clues: _____

_____

Impressed means: _____

_____

_____ Number of Correct Answers: Part B

C Using Words

◆ Cross out one of the four words in each row that does **not** fit with the word in dark type.

1. tournament

    win   sleep   play   enter

2. professional

    walk   work   skill   money

3. amateur

    enjoy   play   hobby   mail

4. qualify

    success   prove   clean   test

5. par

    score   count   number   shake

◆ Choose one of the words shown in dark type above. Write a sentence using the word.

6. word: _____

_____

_____

_____ Number of Correct Answers: Part C

D Writing About It

Write A Comic Strip

◆ Write a comic strip about Michelle Wie. First look at what is happening in each scene. Think about what each person might be saying. Then finish the sentence in each bubble. Use the checklist on page 103 to check your work.

Lesson 4 Add your correct answers from parts A, B, and C to get your total score. Then find the percentage for your total score on the chart below. Record your percentage on the graph on page 105.

_____ Total Score for Parts A, B, and C

_____ Percentage

Total Score	1	2	3	4	5	6	7	8	9	10	11	12	13
Percentage	8	15	23	31	38	46	54	62	69	77	85	92	100

Johnny Depp

Being an Actor Wasn't His Plan

Birth Name John Christopher Depp II

Birth Date and Place June 9, 1963; Owensboro, Kentucky

Home Plan de la Tour and Paris, France

Think About What You Know

If you had to choose, would you rather be a movie star or a famous rock musician? Why? Read the article and find out which career Johnny Depp would have chosen.

Word Power

What do the words below tell you about the article?

appealing likeable or pleasing

miserable very unhappy or not comfortable

artificial not real or not natural

romantic someone who enjoys thoughts and feelings of love

reputation the way people think about someone because of what has happened in the past

Reading Skill

Cause and Effect Many stories and articles show cause and effect. A **cause** tells *why* something happened. An **effect** tells *what* happened. The cause happens first. Then the effect happens. The clue word *because* can help you find the cause. The clue word *so* can help you find the effect.

| Example |

My sister went to the movies yesterday. She saw a scary move. <u>When she went to bed last night she was still scared</u>, so she slept with her light on.

Cause When she went to bed last night she was still scared

Effect she slept with her light on.

The cause in the paragraph is "When she went to bed last night she was still scared." The effect is "she slept with her light on." The word *so* is a clue word to help you find the effect. The words that come after the word *so* usually show the effect. What words come after the word *so* in the paragraph?

Johnny Depp

Being an Actor Wasn't His Plan

Johnny Depp didn't want to be a movie star. What he really wanted was to be a musician. As a teenager he played in more than 15 different bands. None of them lasted. By the age of 20 he was out of work and out of money. A friend told him he should try acting. Depp didn't like the idea. But at last he tried out for the movie *Nightmare on Elm Street* (1984). He got a part. Like it or not, his acting career had begun.

2   *Nightmare on Elm Street* led to other small movie roles. Then Depp was offered a part on the TV show *21 Jump Street*. He would play an undercover police officer. Depp didn't really want to do it. He still wanted to be a musician. On the other hand, he needed the money. He thought the show wouldn't last long. So he decided to do it.

3   To Depp's surprise, the show became a big hit. Teenage girls especially loved it. They liked Depp's character. They also liked his looks. Depp is one quarter Cherokee. He is part Navajo, Irish, and German, as well. Viewers found him very **appealing.** Before he knew it, Johnny Depp had become a favorite with teenagers across the country.

4   Depp wasn't happy about this. In fact he was **miserable.** He did everything he could to get himself fired from the show. He started coming to work dressed in strange clothes. He began talking with an Indian accent. He even tried saying his lines with a rubber band wrapped around his tongue. He hoped his bosses would get tired of him. But it didn't work. They knew he was the reason why the show was such a success. They refused to fire him.

5 After several years, Depp finally left *21 Jump Street*. He was eager to change his image. He didn't want to be known as an ordinary leading man. He definitely didn't want people to think of him as just a pretty face. So Depp made a point of signing up for odd roles. He starred in the movie *Edward Scissorhands* (1990). Here he played an **artificial** man. He appeared with wild black hair, chalk-white skin, and had scissor blades in place of hands.

6 In 1993 Depp starred as the unhappy son of a 500-pound woman in *What's Eating Gilbert Grape?* He also took on the role of a sweet but strange man in *Benny and Joon*. The same year he played someone who heard the dreams of fishes in *Arizona Dream*.

7 It wasn't just that he wanted odd roles. Depp enjoyed playing all sorts of characters. He did not want to be the kind of actor who did the same thing again and again. He was always looking for new roles. So he became the world's greatest **romantic** in *Don Juan DeMarco* (1995). He became a writer with a terrible drug problem in *Fear and Loathing in Las Vegas* (1998). And he turned into a traveling horseman for *The Man Who Cried* (2000).

8 Many of the movies Depp made were dramas. Others were not. He starred in the science fiction tale *The Astronaut's Wife* (1999). He also made a horror movie called *The Ninth Gate* (1999). Then he appeared in the love story *Chocolat* (2000).

Skill Break

Cause and Effect

Look at paragraph 5 on this page. This paragraph shows cause and effect. The **cause** is that Depp did not want to be known as an ordinary actor or someone who just had a pretty face. What is the **effect?**

What **clue word** did you use?

9   As the years went by, Depp got a **reputation** for being a fine actor. Some people said he was the best actor of his time. But he had another reputation as well. He was known as "box-office poison." This meant his films never made much money. People who saw Depp's work understood how good he was. Even so, his films just didn't appeal to that many people.

10   In 2003 that changed. Actually, by 2003 *Depp* had changed. He had become a parent. He and Vanessa Paradis had a daughter, Lily-Rose, in 1999. Their son Jack was born in 2001. Depp loved being a father. After Lily-Rose was born he said, "I feel like there was a fog in front of my eyes for 36 years. The second she was born, that fog just lifted." After Jack was born, Depp said, "Vanessa and my kids have grounded me . . . It feels really good."

11   Depp no longer felt he had to take the wildest and strangest roles he could find. Instead he surprised everyone by saying that he'd "like to do some kiddie stuff." He wanted to make a movie that Lily-Rose and Jack could watch. So he took a role in the movie *Pirates of the Caribbean: The Curse of the Black Pearl* (2003). In it he played a pirate named Jack Sparrow. The movie gave Depp plenty of chances to act crazy. It also let him show how funny he could be. Unlike his other films, this was a movie everyone could love. It was a huge success. Depp was even nominated for an Academy Award. But best of all, his children enjoyed seeing the movie.

Fun Facts

▶ Depp dreamed of becoming a basketball player when he was a boy.

▶ He owns a restaurant in Paris and a place to hear rock bands in Hollywood.

▶ He likes to collect rare books.

Johnny Depp plays a game of pirates in this scene from the movie *Finding Neverland*.

12   After *Pirates* Depp went on to other projects. He was still looking for new challenges. In 2004 he made a scary film called *Secret Window*. Later he made a movie about a poet who lived in the 1600s. It was called *The Libertine*. These movies showed that Depp was still trying to grow as an actor.

13   By this time, Depp was no longer box-office poison. He no longer stayed away from popular films. In fact, he soon made more big hits. One was *Finding Neverland* (2004). It was about the man who wrote the story of Peter Pan. Depp also made *Charlie and the Chocolate Factory* (2005).

14   Depp had learned that being a big star didn't mean he would have to make bad movies. He decided, "I might as well enjoy the ride while I'm on it."

◆ **Fill in the circle next to the correct answer.**

1. Depp tried to get fired from *21 Jump Street* by

    ○ A. pretending he was a pirate.

    ○ B. talking with an Indian accent.

    ○ C. coming to work with messy hair.

2. In which paragraph did you find the information to answer number 1?

    ○ A. paragraph 4

    ○ B. paragraph 6

    ○ C. paragraph 7

3. His role in *Pirates of the Caribbean* allowed Depp to

    ○ A. make his first scary movie.

    ○ B. win an Academy Award.

    ○ C. show that he could be funny.

4. From the information in the article, you can predict that Depp will

    ○ A. get a chance to become a famous musician.

    ○ B. make more movies that his kids can watch.

    ○ C. quit acting and spend more time with his family.

5. The author probably wrote this article in order to

    ○ A. tell the reader about Depp's life and his movies.

    ○ B. explain to the reader why Depp lives in France.

    ○ C. make the reader go to see all of Depp's movies.

_____ Number of Correct Answers: Part A

B Understanding Cause and Effect

◆ Read the paragraph below. The paragraph shows cause and effect. The cause is that Depp's bosses knew he was the reason why the show was a success. Fill in the circle next to the sentence that shows the **effect**.

1.

    Depp wasn't happy about this. In fact he was miserable. He did everything he could to get himself fired from the show. He started coming to work dressed in strange clothes. He began talking with an Indian accent. He even tried saying his lines with a rubber band wrapped around his tongue. He hoped his bosses would get tired of him. But it didn't work. They knew he was the reason why the show was such a success. They refused to fire him.

○ A. They made him miserable.
○ B. They got tired of him.
○ C. They refused to fire him.

◆ Reread paragraph 11 in the article. The paragraph shows cause and effect. The cause is that Depp wanted to make a movie that his kids could watch. Write the **effect** below. Then write the clue word that helped you find the effect.

2. Effect: _____

_____

Clue Word: _____

_____ Number of Correct Answers: Part B

C Using Words

Complete each sentence with a word from the box. Write the missing word on the line.

appealing	artificial	reputation
miserable	romantic	

1. She felt _____ while she had the flu.

2. The _____ plant looked so green that I had to touch it to see if it was real.

3. She has a _____ for getting good grades.

4. The love poems he wrote showed he was a _____.

5. Many people came to hear the singer's _____ voice.

Choose one of the words from the box. Write a new sentence using the word.

6. word: _____

_____

_____

_____ Number of Correct Answers: Part C

D Writing About It

Write a Postcard

◆ Write a postcard to Johnny Depp. Finish the sentences below to write your postcard. Use the checklist on page 103 to check your work.

Dear Mr. Depp,

    I just read an article about you. I liked reading about_____

_____.

I was surprised when I read that _____

_____.

I hope you will _____

_____.

                Sincerely,

            _____

Mr. Johnny Depp
234 Depp Ln.
Johnnyville, USA

Lesson 5 Add your correct answers from parts A, B, and C to get your total score. Then find the percentage for your total score on the chart below. Record your percentage on the graph on page 105.

_____ Total Score for Parts A, B, and C

_____ Percentage

Total Score	1	2	3	4	5	6	7	8	9	10	11	12	13
Percentage	8	15	23	31	38	46	54	62	69	77	85	92	100

Tim McGraw

Music Man and Family Man

Full Name Samuel Timothy McGraw

Birth Date and Place May 1, 1967; Delhi, Louisiana

Home Nashville, Tennessee

Think About What You Know

What do you think makes a person a good parent? Read the article and find out how Tim McGraw feels about being a father.

Word Power

What do the words below tell you about the article?

certificate a paper which lists the facts about something

luxury a state of being very comfortable and having everything you want

abandoning leaving something or someone behind

issue to give

priority something that's important or that needs to come first

Reading Skill

Making Predictions A **prediction** is a good guess about what will happen later in a story or an article. Good readers make predictions based on clues from the text and what they already know. Good readers change their predictions as they read more of the story or article.

| Example |

> People began filling the seats in front of the concert-hall stage. As the last seats were being taken, the stage lights came up. Everyone in the hall began to clap and cheer.

From the information in the paragraph you can predict that *a band is going to give a concert*. One clue to make this prediction is "People began filling the seats in front of the concert-hall stage." What other clues tell you that a show is about to begin? How does what you already know help you use these clues?

Tim McGraw

Music Man and Family Man

Eleven-year-old Timothy Smith was looking through a box of family photos when he found something very surprising. Tucked among the photos was his birth **certificate.** It told when and where he had been born. It also gave the names of his parents. His mom, Betty Trimble, was listed as "Mother." But his dad, Horace Smith, did not appear as "Father." A different name was there instead. It was Tug McGraw, the famous relief pitcher for the Philadelphia Phillies.

2   Tim could hardly believe it. But it was true. Betty Trimble and Tug McGraw had never married. Tug had never been part of Tim's life. Betty had moved to Louisiana and married Horace Smith when Tim was just seven months old. She had let Tim think Horace was his only father.

3   Learning the truth was hard on Tim. He made a trip to Philadelphia and met Tug. But Tug didn't want Tim in his life. So while Tug lived a life of **luxury,** Tim and his mother struggled through hard times. During Tim's early years, Horace Smith had worked as a truck driver to help pay the bills. But Horace had left Betty when Tim was nine. Since then Betty had been on her own.

4   "She worked two or three jobs at a time," says Tim. "I can remember being 11-, 12-, 13-years-old and getting up at 12:00 at night." His mother would be "sitting at the kitchen table with the bills spread out everywhere . . . with her head down crying." The next day the VCR or some other item would be gone, sold to pay the rent or the electric bill.

5   When Tim finished high school in 1985, there was no money for college. That's when Betty finally turned to Tug for help. Tim wanted to go to Northeast Louisiana University. Would Tug help pay for it?

6   Tug agreed to help Tim pay for college. He also said he would meet with Tim one more time. After that he wanted Tim out of his life forever. Tug was worried that Tim was after his money. He thought Tim might cause trouble for him. So when they met, Tug asked Tim what he wanted. Tim said, "I just need somebody that I can call 'Dad.'" With those words, Tug finally understood. It wasn't about money. It was about family.

7   Slowly Tim and Tug began to build a friendship. Tim was willing to forget the past. He was willing to forgive Tug for **abandoning** him. Over the next 15 years, he and Tug managed to become good friends. Tim even took the name McGraw as his own last name.

8   Meanwhile Tim headed off to college. While there he fell in love with country music. He had grown up listening to country musicians like Merle Haggard and Charlie Rich. Now he didn't just want to listen, he wanted to play. He bought a second-hand guitar for $20. Then he sat down and taught himself to play it.

Skill Break
Making Predictions
Look at paragraph 8 on this page. This paragraph tells about what happened when McGraw went to college. Using clues in the paragraph, what do you think is most likely to **happen next?**

What **clues** did you use to make your prediction?

How does **what you already know** help you use the clues?

As you read the next page, check to see if what happens next matches your prediction.

9   In 1989 Tim moved to Nashville. He formed a band and began playing in bars. These were not fancy clubs. Some of the people who played with the band remember just how dangerous the places were. One says, "They'd tell us, 'Oh yeah, last week three people got shot here.'" Another says, "You'd have chicken wire up in front of the stage, so that people couldn't throw bottles at you." A third band member remembers, "Some of the times if you didn't have a gun or a knife, they would **issue** you one at the door."

10   Tim McGraw didn't mind. He was just happy to be making music. He signed a contract with Curb Records in 1991. His first album came out a year later. It didn't do well. Then in 1994 his second album came out. It contained the song "Not a Moment Too Soon." This became a big hit. The album sold five million copies. Suddenly Tim McGraw was famous.

11   From then on, McGraw's life just got better and better. He became a huge star. It wasn't just country music fans who loved him. His songs were also popular with pop and R & B music fans. In 2004 his song "Live Like You Were Dying" spent eight weeks at the top of the charts. It also won him a Grammy Award. Sadly, Tug McGraw died of cancer just before this song was recorded. For Tim McGraw, who had nursed his father through his final months of life, the song had special meaning.

Fun Facts

▸ McGraw enjoys fishing and cooking.

▸ In 2004 he recorded a hit song with rapper Nelly called "Over and Over."

▸ He sometimes records his music in a studio on the top of a mountain in New York.

Tim McGraw sings at the 2004 Country Music Awards. He won the award for best song of the year.

12   Tim McGraw married country music star Faith Hill in 1996. By 2005 they had three daughters. McGraw knew from experience how important it was for a child to have a father. He made sure to spend lots of time with his children. "My kids and my family are my number-one **priority**," he says. "There's not even a close second." He sets up his schedule so that he never has to be away from them for long. A national fatherhood group even gave him the Father of the Year Award in 2000.

13   In 2004 McGraw began acting in movies. He appeared in *Friday Night Lights*. The next year he took on a starring role in the film *My Friend Flicka*. McGraw loves making movies, but music is still his real calling. As he puts it, "I'm not going to quit my day job."

14   Tim McGraw knows how lucky he is, so he tries to help those who are not so lucky. He has raised money for the Red Cross. He has helped families of soldiers killed while at war. He has helped hurricane victims and cancer patients, and has supported Little League teams. In many ways, Tim McGraw has shown that he cares. He has made a difference in the lives of many people.

Understanding What You Read

◆ **Fill in the circle next to the correct answer.**

1. As a child, Tim didn't know Tug McGraw was his father because

○ A. Tug McGraw was traveling a lot.

○ B. Tim's mother never told him about Tug.

○ C. Tim never watched Tug's baseball games.

2. Choose the statement below that states an opinion.

○ A. He moved to Nashville.

○ B. He is the greatest father ever.

○ C. He won a Grammy Award.

3. From what you read in the article, which of these is probably true?

○ A. McGraw will start to make more movies and fewer records.

○ B. McGraw tries to see Horace Smith as often as possible.

○ C. McGraw is usually with his family when he isn't working.

4. McGraw wants to help other people because

○ A. he knows how lucky he is.

○ B. he is a good father.

○ C. he has won many awards.

5. Which sentence **best** states the lesson about life that this article teaches?

○ A. You can share your happiness by helping others.

○ B. You should take your time when making decisions.

○ C. You need to practice if you want to be good at something.

_____ Number of Correct Answers: Part A

B Making Predictions

◆ Read the paragraphs below. Look at the clues in the paragraphs. Fill in the circle next to the prediction that is **most likely** to happen based on the clues.

1.

Eleven-year-old Timothy Smith was looking through a box of family photos when he found something very surprising. Tucked among the photos was his birth certificate. It told when and where he had been born. It also told who his parents were. His mom, Betty Trimble, was listed as "Mother." But his dad, Horace Smith, did not appear as "Father." A different name was there instead. It was Tug McGraw, the famous relief pitcher for the Philadelphia Phillies.

Tim could hardly believe it. But it was true. Betty Trimble and Tug McGraw had never married. Tug had never been part of Tim's life. Betty had moved to Louisiana and married Horace Smith when Tim was just seven months old. She had let Tim think Horace was his only father.

○ A. Tim will want to meet Tug McGraw.
○ B. Tim will forget about what he saw in the box.
○ C. Tim will become a famous baseball player.

◆ What clues in the paragraphs above helped you make the prediction? How did what you already know help you make the prediction? Write the clues and what you already know on the lines.

2. Clues: _____

What I Know: _____

_____ Number of Correct Answers: Part B

61

C Using Words

◆ Cross out one of the four words in each row that does **not** fit with the word in dark type.

1. certificate

record   information   laugh   date

2. luxury

clothes   houses   cars   thoughts

3. abandoning

cook   lose   distant   gone

4. issue

give   run   offer   share

5. priority

first   main   empty   highest

◆ Choose one of the words shown in dark type above. Write a new sentence using the word.

6. word: _____

_____

_____

_____ Number of Correct Answers: Part C

62

D Writing About It

Write a Scene from a Play

◆ Write a scene from a play about Tim and Tug McGraw. The scene takes place when Tug meets with Tim before Tim goes to college. Finish the sentences below to write your scene. Use the checklist on page 103 to check your work.

(Tim and Tug are sitting at a table in a coffee shop.)

Tim: I'm glad you agreed to meet with me today.

Tug: I'm already helping you pay for college. What more do you

want? I'm worried that _____

_____ .

Tim: Don't worry. I don't want _____

_____ .

Tug: What do you want then?

Tim: I just want _____ .

Lesson 6 Add your correct answers from parts A, B, and C to get your total score. Then find the percentage for your total score on the chart below. Record your percentage on the graph on page 105.

_____ Total Score for Parts A, B, and C

_____ Percentage

Total Score	1	2	3	4	5	6	7	8	9	10	11	12	13
Percentage	8	15	23	31	38	46	54	62	69	77	85	92	100

Compare and Contrast

◆ Think about the celebrities, or famous people, in Unit Two. Pick two articles that tell about celebrities who made decisions that affected their families. Use information from the articles to fill in this chart.

Celebrity's Name		
What decision did the celebrity make?		
Why did the celebrity make this decision?		
How did the decision affect the celebrity's family?		

Jennifer Lopez

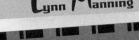

Lynn Manning

Aaron McGruder

Jennifer Lopez

Living a Superstar's Life

Birth Name Jennifer Lynn Lopez

Birth Date and Place July 24, 1969; the Bronx, New York City

Home Miami, Florida, and several other cities

Think About What You Know

Have you ever worked hard to get what you wanted? What were your challenges? Read the article and find out what Jennifer Lopez did to become a superstar.

Word Power

What do the words below tell you about the article?

glamorous full of beauty and excitement

trials difficult tests of a person's inner strength

ultimate greatest

gossip talk about the personal business of other people, often in a mean way

privacy freedom from being watched or bothered by other people

Reading Skill

Using Context **Context clues** can help you find the meaning of a word that you don't understand. Context clues are other words in the same sentence or in nearby sentences. If you don't understand a word, look for clues around it that might help you. Then try to find the meaning.

| Example |

On the night of the awards ceremony, the movie star wore her finest dress. She knew that her outfit would be

New Word

carefully scrutinized. Since people were watching, she wanted to look her best. If people liked what they saw, her

Context Clues

picture would be in all the fashion magazines.

If you don't know the meaning of the word *scrutinized,* you can use the context clues "carefully," "people were watching," and "what they saw" to help you find the meaning. From these clues, what do you think *scrutinized* means?

Jennifer Lopez
Living a Superstar's Life

Most people think Jennifer Lopez has it made. After all, she is a huge star. She has made hit movies and record albums. She has plenty of money, with her wealth adding up to more than $250 million. If that's not enough, Jennifer Lopez, or "J. Lo" as she's often called, is beautiful. Again and again she has been named one of the 50 most beautiful people in the world by *People* magazine. So it may be surprising to hear Lopez say, "There have been times when I didn't want to be me anymore. From the outside looking in, it may have appeared that it was a **glamorous,** exciting life, but I would have swapped places with anybody."

2   To understand why Lopez said this, it helps to think about the many **trials** she has faced. The first one was simply surviving in the part of town where she grew up. It was a tough section of the Bronx in New York City. "Don't get caught here after dark," says one man who still lives there. "I've seen two guys shot to death a couple of blocks from the Lopez house. There are drug deals everywhere."

3   Lopez's parents worked hard to keep their daughter safe. They sent her to private school. They also started her on singing and dancing lessons when she was five. To keep their eye on her, they encouraged her to practice in the living room. There she listened to all sorts of music. She says she watched the musical *West Side Story* over 100 times.

4   Fortunately, Lopez was able to get through her childhood years unharmed. Her next challenge would be launching, or starting, a career. Lopez's parents hoped she would become a lawyer. While in college, Lopez did work in a law office. She really wanted to be an entertainer, though. So she moved to California and tried to get work as a dancer. She went to many try-outs. It took months of going to auditions before she had much luck. At last in 1991, she became a dancer on the TV show *In Living Color*.

5   After that Lopez started acting. She got small roles in TV movies and Hollywood films. People began to notice what a fine actress she was. Film makers began giving her more important roles. Then came her big break. She was picked to star in the movie *Selena* (1997). This film required Lopez to sing as well as act. "Singing never seemed like a risk to me," she says. Then she adds, "I know people had their doubts."

6   Lopez is right. People did have doubts. Lopez dazzled everyone, though. Tommy Mottola is the head of a large music company. He says, "I knew she could dance, and I knew she could act. Once I heard her sing, I thought, 'Man, here she is, the **ultimate** superstar.'" After *Selena* came out, Lopez signed a record contract with Mottola's company.

Skill Break

Using Context

Look at paragraph 4 on this page. Find the word *auditions* near the end of the paragraph.

What **clues** in the paragraph can help you find the meaning of *auditions*?

From the clues, what do you think *auditions* means?

7   Lopez had indeed become a superstar. She put out one best-selling music album after another. She made big films such as *Out of Sight* (1998) and *The Wedding Planner* (2001). She got into fashion design and created her own line of clothing. She even started her own production company. Lopez called it *Nuyorican,* which is what many Puerto Rican New Yorkers call themselves. She did this to honor her hometown and her family's Puerto Rican background. In 2001 Lopez became the first woman to have both a movie *and* an album reach number one on the charts in the same week.

8   Being a superstar doesn't mean that life is easy for Lopez, though. She works very, very hard. She often works 14 hours a day on a movie set. Then she goes to a recording studio to work on her music. So even though she owns beautiful homes, she hasn't had much time to enjoy them.

9   There is another price Lopez has paid for her success. People watch every move she makes. They notice every mistake. And they don't stop talking about her. They **gossip** about her constantly. One thing they talk about is her love life.

10   Lopez had two marriages that didn't last long. She also had some famous boyfriends. One was rap star Sean "Diddy" Combs. Another was actor Ben Affleck. All of these relationships were watched closely by the public. Endless pictures were taken. Countless stories were written. In 2004 Lopez married Latin superstar Marc Anthony, and the pictures and stories kept coming. Lopez's love life has become a source of entertainment for people.

Fun Facts

▶ As a young girl, Lopez was good at tennis and softball.

▶ Her favorite meal is chicken with red beans and rice.

▶ Before Lopez became famous, she worked for Janet Jackson as a background dancer.

Famous actor Jennifer Lopez is also a talented dancer and singer.

11 "Everybody has laughed," she says. "It hurts, it always does."

12 Everyone also seems to have a Jennifer Lopez story to tell. One is that she won't ride in a silver limousine if she ordered a gray one. Another is that she won't stay in a hotel room unless the sheets are made from a certain kind of cotton. Lopez denies these stories. She says that much of what people say about her is "crazy." She tries not to pay attention to them. But she knows that every day people are talking about her. She also knows that much of what they say is mean and untrue.

13 Lopez is not complaining. She enjoys the life she has chosen. But she would like to find some balance in her life. She would like a little more free time, and she would like a bit of **privacy.** So while she doesn't regret the decisions she has made, she has plans to make the future even better. She feels that she will always be changing and improving. "I'm a work in progress," she says. "You learn as you go. Everything is just a lesson to get you to the next place."

Understanding What You Read

◆ **Fill in the circle next to the correct answer.**

1. Choose the statement below that states an opinion.

○ A. Lopez grew up in New York.

○ B. Lopez has made hit movies.

○ C. Lopez is very beautiful.

2. What was the cause of Lopez moving to California?

○ A. She was accepted into law school.

○ B. She wanted to be an entertainer.

○ C. She was hired to star in the movie *Selena*.

3. In which paragraph did you find the information to answer question 2?

○ A. paragraph 3

○ B. paragraph 4

○ C. paragraph 5

4. Lopez named her production company *Nuyorican* after a

○ A. commonly used term for Puerto Rican New Yorkers.

○ B. famous Puerto Rican restaurant in New York.

○ C. large Puerto Rican neighborhood in the Bronx.

5. The many stories that people tell about Lopez

○ A. make her laugh.

○ B. hurt her feelings.

○ C. help her work.

_____ Number of Correct Answers: Part A

B Using Context

◆ Read the paragraph below. Look for context clues that tell you what the word *limousine* means. Underline the context clues in the paragraph. Then fill in the circle next to the correct meaning of *limousine*.

1.

Everyone also seems to have a Jennifer Lopez story to tell. One is that she won't ride in a silver limousine if she ordered a gray one. Another is that she won't stay in a hotel room unless the sheets are made from a certain kind of cotton. Lopez denies these stories. She says that much of what people say about her is "crazy." She tries not to pay attention to them. But she knows that every day people are talking about her. She also knows that much of what they say is mean and untrue.

○ A. a car with a hired driver
○ B. a special kind of blanket
○ C. an elevator in a large hotel

◆ Reread paragraph 13 in the article. Find the word *progress* near the end of the paragraph. Look for context clues about the meaning of *progress*. Write the clues on the lines below. Then write what you think *progress* means.

2. Context Clue: _____

Progress means: _____

_____

_____ Number of Correct Answers: Part B

C Using Words

◆ The words and phrases in the list below relate to the words in the box. Some words or phrases in the list have a meaning that is the same as or similar to a word in the box. Some have the opposite meaning. Write the related word from the box on each line. Use each word from the box twice.

glamorous	ultimate	privacy
trials	gossip	

Same or similar meaning

1. challenges _____

2. time alone _____

3. thrilling _____

4. best _____

5. spread rumors _____

Opposite meaning

6. keep secrets _____

7. easy times _____

8. dull _____

9. company _____

10. worst _____

_____ Number of Correct Answers: Part C

D Writing About It

Write a Magazine Article

◆ Suppose you are a reporter who writes about famous people. Write a magazine article about Jennifer Lopez and her career. Finish the sentences below to write your article. Use the checklist on page 103 to check your work.

Lopez's first entertainment job was _____

_____.

After her success in the movie *Selena,* Lopez became a huge star. In

addition to her movies, she also _____,

and _____.

People may think her life is easy. The truth is _____

_____.

Lesson 7 Add your correct answers from parts A, B, and C to get your total score. Then find the percentage for your total score on the chart below. Record your percentage on the graph on page 105.

_____ Total Score for Parts A, B, and C

_____ Percentage

Total Score	1	2	3	4	5	6	7	8	9	10	11	12	13	14	15	16	17
Percentage	6	12	18	24	29	35	41	47	53	59	65	71	76	82	88	94	100

Lynn Manning
Dealing with Loss

Birth Name Lynn Manning

Birth Date and Place April 30, 1955; Fresno, California

Home Los Angeles, California

Think About What You Know

Do you think difficult experiences can make you a stronger person? How? Read the article and find out how Lynn Manning's experiences changed him.

Word Power

What do the words below tell you about the article?

abusive harmful to other people

recovery a return to health after being sick or hurt

judo a sport like wrestling, in which the athletes try to tip each other over

consultant someone whose job is to give helpful information

believable accepted as true or real

Reading Skill

Cause and Effect Many stories and articles show cause and effect. A **cause** tells *why* something happened. An **effect** tells *what* happened. The cause happens first. Then the effect happens. Sometimes you will have to find the cause or the effect without the help of clue words. You can ask the question *Why did this happen?* to find the cause. Ask *What happened as a result?* to find the effect.

Example

Cause	The artist was ready to begin a new painting. She decided to paint a sunset. She began painting every
Effect	day while the sun went down.

The cause in the paragraph is "She decided to paint a sunset." The effect is "She began painting every day as the sun went down." To find the cause you can ask, *Why did she paint while the sun went down?* What question can you ask to find the effect?

Lynn Manning

Dealing with Loss

Lynn Manning expected bad things to happen. It wasn't that he looked for trouble. It was just that nothing in his life happened the way he hoped. When he was a small boy, Manning's life seemed peaceful. When he was eight, though, his family was torn apart. His father became **abusive** and eventually left their Los Angeles home. Soon his mother's serious drinking problem made her unable to take care of her children.

2   Manning and his eight brothers and sisters had to take care of themselves. Sometimes their mother would disappear for days at a time, leaving almost nothing in the house for the children to eat. Manning ate margarine and sugar sandwiches. "It was hard," he recalls. "It was real hard."

3   Finally state officials got involved and sent the children to foster homes. Manning was moved from one foster family to the next. At the age of 16, he was sent to the McCobb Home for Boys. By then he had learned not to get attached to anything around him, including schools, neighborhoods, and people. "I was just used to having things snatched away from me," he says.

4   One thing Manning held onto was his dream of being an artist. His stepfather had taught him to draw and paint when he was a little boy. Manning had been doing art ever since. He hoped to live in Paris and make a living by selling paintings. So at age 18, he went to college to study art. He had an eerie feeling, though. Everything he had ever loved had been taken away from him. What if the same thing happened with painting? What if he somehow lost his sight?

5   He had no reason to think he would lose his vision, but he prepared for it anyway. He practiced washing dishes with his eyes closed. He dialed the telephone in the dark. He kept studying to be an artist, but he said, "The way things have been going in my life, you know, it might not happen."

6   By the time Manning was 23, it seemed he had left his bad luck behind him. His paintings were getting better and better. He was making money by working at the McCobb Home for Boys. In fact, on October 25, 1978, Manning was given the job of house director. To celebrate, he went to his favorite bar. That's when Manning's worst nightmare came true.

7   A man in the bar tried to pick a fight with him. Manning ignored him but the man wouldn't stop. Finally Manning grabbed the man and threw him out of the bar. Within an hour the man returned carrying a gun. He walked up to Manning and shot him in the head. The bullet destroyed Manning's left eye and cut the nerve to his right eye. As a result, it left him completely without sight. Like everything else, his dream of being a painter had now been "snatched away."

Skill Break
Cause and Effect
Look at paragraph 2 on page 78. This paragraph shows cause and effect. The cause is that their mother would disappear for days at a time. What is the **effect?**

What **question** did you ask to help you find the effect?

8   Although Manning's fears had come true, he refused to give up on life. The practicing he had done before the shooting helped him make a swift **recovery.** In addition, he learned to read braille. He also learned how to walk alone by tapping with a cane. "It feels a little dorky at first, but I catch on," he says. "I've got natural rhythm. I'll figure a way to make it look cool later."

9   Manning's doctors couldn't believe how quickly he bounced back. "I'm used to loss," he told them. "So I'm a fast learner." Just eight months after the shooting, Manning had gone back to college and was living on his own again.

10   At 6 feet 2 inches, Manning had always had a strong body. He didn't want to lose it just because he was unable to see. So he started learning **judo,** a sport that uses quick moves to tip an opponent over. He became so good that in 1990 he won the Blind Judo World Championship. The United States Olympic Committee named him "Blind Male Athlete of the Year." A year later in Italy, Manning won the first World Cup for blind judo. Today he no longer competes, but he still teaches judo to blind students.

Fun **F**acts

▶ Manning enjoys playing music on the harmonica.

▶ He wrote and starred in a short film called *Shoot.*

▶ Sometimes he uses a special computer program to help him read. The program changes text into speech so he can listen to the words.

Lynn Manning won two blind judo championships in the 1990s. Today he teaches judo to people who are blind.

11   Because Manning could no longer be a painter, he worked on a different art: writing. His poems began to appear in major magazines. He also started writing plays. One of his best plays is called *Weights*. It is a one-man play about Manning's own life or, as he says, how he went "from black man to blind man." Manning plays himself in *Weights*. He uses storytelling, poetry, and music. *Weights* has won three Theater Awards from the National Association for the Advancement of Colored People (NAACP).

12   In 2005 Manning became a **consultant** for the TV show *Blind Justice.* The show featured a police officer returning to duty after losing his vision. Manning helped actor Ron Eldard understand what it is like to live without sight. He helped make Eldard's character more **believable.**

13   Lynn Manning is now in his 50s, but he has no plans to slow down. He has new projects in mind. He volunteers his time to work with disabled persons. He recently got married too. His life is full, and that's just the way Lynn Manning likes it.

A Understanding What You Read

◆ Fill in the circle next to the correct answer.

1. When Manning was given the job of house director at the McCobb Home, he

○ A. went to his favorite bar to celebrate.

○ B. knew he could not be a painter anymore.

○ C. decided to quit college and live on his own.

2. If you could not see, how might you use the information in the article to help you plan your career?

○ A. I would call Manning and ask for a job.

○ B. I would think about becoming a writer.

○ C. I would start taking art lessons.

3. The TV show *Blind Justice* is about

○ A. Manning's own life after he was shot.

○ B. a person who teaches blind students.

○ C. a police officer who has lost his sight.

4. How is Lynn Manning an example of a brave person?

○ A. He has a strong body.

○ B. He did not give up after he lost his sight.

○ C. He no longer has to worry about having enough food.

5. From the information in the article, you can predict that Manning will

○ A. get his sight back.

○ B. win another World Cup.

○ C. write more plays.

_____ Number of Correct Answers: Part A

◆ Read the paragraph below. The paragraph shows cause and effect. The cause is that Manning was moved from one foster family to the next. Fill in the circle next to the sentence that shows the **effect.**

1.

Finally state officials got involved and sent the children to foster homes. Manning was moved from one foster family to the next. At the age of 16, he was sent to the McCobb Home for Boys. By then he had learned not to get attached to anything around him, including schools, neighborhoods, and people. "I was just used to having things snatched away from me," he says.

○ A. State officials got involved in Manning's life.
○ B. Manning learned not to get attached to anything.
○ C. Neighbors took things from Manning.

◆ Reread paragraphs 4 and 5 in the article. The paragraphs show cause and effect. The cause is that Manning had an eerie feeling. What question can you ask to find the **effect?** Write the question and the effect on the lines below.

2. Question: _____

_____

Effect: _____

_____

_____ Number of Correct Answers: Part B

C   Using Words

◆ Cross out one of the four words in each row that does **not** relate to the word in dark type.

1. abusive

| pain | afraid | swim | protect |

2. recovery

| ill | paper | hurt | better |

3. judo

| wash | struggle | strength | athlete |

4. consultant

| luck | help | expert | listen |

5. believable

| details | trust | story | sick |

◆ Choose one of the words shown in dark type above. Write a sentence using the word.

6. word: _____

_____

_____

_____ Number of Correct Answers: Part C

D Writing About It

Write an Advertisement

◆ Write an advertisement for Lynn Manning's play *Weights*. Finish the sentences below to write your advertisement. Use the checklist on page 103 to check your work.

Tickets on Sale

See Lynn Manning Perform in *Weights*

Tickets on Sale

Lynn Manning's play, *Weights*, is a one-man play about _____

_____

_____.

Manning's play won_____

_____.

The story of *Weights* is inspiring because Manning _____

_____.

Lesson 8 Add your correct answers from parts A, B, and C to get your total score. Then find the percentage for your total score on the chart below. Record your percentage on the graph on page 105.

_____ Total Score for Parts A, B, and C

_____ Percentage

Total Score	1	2	3	4	5	6	7	8	9	10	11	12	13
Percentage	8	15	23	31	38	46	54	62	69	77	85	92	100

Aaron McGruder

Writing a New Kind of Comic Strip

Birth Name Aaron McGruder

Birth Date and Place January 13, 1975; Chicago, Illinois

Home Los Angeles, California

Think About What You Know

Do you ever read comic strips? Which comic strips do you like? Read the article to find out about Aaron McGruder and the comic strip he created.

Word Power

What do the words below tell you about the article?

cynical believing that most people do things for themselves, not for others

suburbs towns that are close to a city but aren't as busy as a city

conservative against change or not liking new ideas

cartoonists people who create cartoons

moral concerned with being good and doing the right thing

Reading Skill

Making Predictions A **prediction** is a good guess about what will happen later in a story or an article. Good readers make predictions based on clues from the text and what they already know. Good readers change their predictions as they read more of the story or article.

Example

My uncle works a lot. He works seven days a week. He doesn't get much sleep at night. He doesn't eat regular meals either. The last time I saw him, he didn't look very healthy.

From the information in the paragraph you can predict that *the uncle might get sick from working so much.* One clue to make this prediction is "The last time I saw him he didn't look very healthy." What other clues tell you that the uncle might get sick? How does what you already know help you use these clues?

Aaron McGruder
Writing a New Kind of Comic Strip

Aaron McGruder has two goals. One is to make people laugh. The other is to make people think. While he may not always succeed with the first goal, he definitely does with the second one.

2   McGruder created the comic strip *The Boondocks*. He began working on it when he was still in college. McGruder had always liked to draw, and he had a lot to say about the world around him. A comic strip seemed like a good way to put these two interests together. In 1996 while still at the University of Maryland, McGruder started drawing *The Boondocks.* At first the strip appeared only in his college newspaper. Within a few months, though, it was being printed in other newspapers. By the time McGruder was 25, almost 200 papers across the country were printing his comic strip.

3   *The Boondocks* features two African American brothers named Huey and Riley. Huey is smart and **cynical.** He reads a lot and makes comments on everything he sees. Riley, meanwhile, is trying to be a rapper. The boys come from inner-city Chicago. They have moved out to the **suburbs** to live with their grandfather, who is grumpy, tired, and more **conservative** than Huey and Riley. The brothers try to take what they know about life in the inner city and apply it to life in the suburbs. Their efforts, and the way their grandfather responds to them, create some very funny scenes.

4   *The Boondocks* is different from most comic strips. This is partly because McGruder is different. McGruder is young and African American, and few well-known **cartoonists** are either of these things.

5   There is another difference as well. Most cartoonists write about safe subjects, such as the small matters of daily life. They play with words and make harmless jokes. Some cartoonists tell cute stories about families and friendships. From the beginning, McGruder wanted to do more. He felt that his comic strip should talk about things that are really important. He wanted to make his readers think about their beliefs and values. As he puts it, "I want to do stuff that has a **moral** center, stuff that I can be proud of."

6   In his early comic strips, McGruder used Huey and Riley's characters to show how unfair some people can be to each other. McGruder used the character of Granddad to get people to take a closer look at themselves. He wanted people to see that they were making bad choices and picking poor role models. As McGruder says, he wanted to show "the things that . . . people don't want to hear about themselves."

7   McGruder's plan wasn't to lecture people. He wanted to make his point with humor. He says, "If you're in the entertainment business and you're trying to get a message across, you have to be entertaining first." So he worked hard to make *The Boondocks* funny. In general he succeeded. Some people found his work upsetting, but many more found it amusing.

8   McGruder liked being successful. But as time passed he began to feel as though he had taken on too much. He spent hours each day trying to think of a funny strip that also had a deeper meaning.

Fun Facts

▶ When he was growing up, McGruder's favorite comic strip was *Peanuts*.

▶ His drawing style is inspired by the popular Japanese style of drawing called manga.

He had trouble finishing his work on time. The work never seemed to end, either. "Seven strips a week," he says. "It's a full-time job with no vacation." The pressure began to affect him. At one point he was suffering so much that he went to the hospital.

9   Then came September 11, 2001. This was the day the United States was attacked. In the weeks that followed, McGruder found new energy. He also found a new direction for his comic strip. He still wanted to make people think about their values. But he began to focus on politics more and more.

10   Most cartoonists stay away from politics. They are afraid of losing their readers and making enemies. McGruder knew this, but he had strong beliefs. He had opinions about U.S. leaders and the war in Iraq. He wanted to share his opinions with readers. He knew he was taking a big chance, but he felt it was worth it. McGruder says, "I decided that I was going to risk throwing my career away. I absolutely thought that was the risk I was taking."

11   Twenty million people a day read *The Boondocks*. McGruder didn't expect them all to like the new direction he was taking. His goal wasn't to bully people into changing their minds. Instead, he said, "The strip is more about challenging people to think differently than they normally do."

Skill Break
Making Predictions
Look at paragraphs 10 and 11 on this page. These paragraphs describe the risk McGruder took when he shared his opinions with his readers. Using clues in the paragraphs, what do you think is most likely to **happen next?**

What **clues** did you use to make your prediction?

How does **what you already know** help you use the clues?

As you read the next page, check to see if what happens next matches your prediction.

Aaron McGruder sits in the studio where many of his *Boondocks* comic strips are created.

12   McGruder's new work did make enemies. Some newspapers even decided to stop printing *The Boondocks*. Even so, most of his readers supported him.

13   Today McGruder is a bigger success than ever. *The Boondocks* appears in more than 300 newspapers. McGruder no longer does his own drawings. An artist in Boston does them for him. Still, McGruder has to think up and write each strip. He has also written a book called *Birth of a Nation: A Comic Novel*. He has created a TV show based on his *Boondocks* characters. McGruder often speaks to college students and other groups too.

14   Aaron McGruder may not make everyone happy, but he certainly gets people's attention. Whether his readers love his work or hate it, they are forced to think about important things. McGruder hopes most readers will do their thinking with smiles on their faces.

A Understanding What You Read

◆ Fill in the circle next to the correct answer.

1. McGruder created *The Boondocks*

○ A. before he moved to inner city Chicago.
○ B. while he was at the University of Maryland.
○ C. after the United States was attacked in 2001.

2. *The Boondocks* is different from most comic strips because it

○ A. makes people think about serious issues.
○ B. is printed seven days a week.
○ C. talks about families and friendships.

3. Some newspapers decided to stop carrying *The Boondocks* because McGruder began to

○ A. have someone else do his drawings for him.
○ B. create new stories for a *Boondocks* TV show.
○ C. show his opinions about U.S. leaders.

4. The author probably wrote this article in order to

○ A. tell the reader about a famous cartoonist.
○ B. make the reader think differently about Chicago.
○ C. show the reader how easy it is to create a comic strip.

5. Which sentence **best** states the main idea of the article?

○ A. McGruder doesn't mind taking risks in his career.
○ B. McGruder created a comic strip that makes people think.
○ C. McGruder has written a book and created a TV show.

_____ Number of Correct Answers: Part A

B Making Predictions

◆ Read the paragraph below. Look at the clues in the paragraph. Fill in the circle next to the prediction that is **most likely** to happen based on the clues.

1.

McGruder liked being successful. But as time passed he began to feel as though he had taken on too much. He spent hours each day trying to think of a funny strip that also had a deeper meaning. He had trouble finishing his work on time. The work never seemed to end, either. "Seven strips a week," he says. "It's a full-time job with no vacation." The pressure began to affect him. At one point he was suffering so much that he went to the hospital.

○ A. McGruder will start finishing his work on time.
○ B. McGruder will draw each comic strip more carefully.
○ C. McGruder will do something to take off some of the pressure.

◆ What clues in the paragraph above helped you make the prediction? How did what you already know help you make the prediction? Write the clues and what you already know on the lines.

2. Clues: _____

_____

What I Know: _____

_____

_____ Number of Correct Answers: Part B

C Using Words

◆ The words and phrases in the list below relate to the words in the box. Some words or phases in the list have a meaning that is the same as or similar to the word in the box. Some have the opposite meaning. Write the related word from the box on each line. Use each word from the box twice.

cynical	conservative	moral
suburbs	cartoonists	

Same or similar meaning

1. artists _____

2. doubting _____

3. neighborhoods _____

4. careful _____

5. picture makers _____

6. honest _____

7. towns _____

Opposite meaning

8. always changing _____

9. bad _____

10. trusting _____

_____ Number of Correct Answers: Part C

D Writing About It

Write a Speech

◆ Write a speech about Aaron McGruder and why his work is important. Finish the sentences below to write your speech. Use the checklist on page 103 to check your work.

Aaron McGruder has changed the way people think about

comic strips. He is different from other cartoonists because _____

_____.

McGruder's comic strip, *The Boondocks,* is about _____

_____.

The Boondocks makes people laugh. It also makes people think

because _____

_____.

Lesson 9 Add your correct answers from parts A, B, and C to get your total score. Then find the percentage for your total score on the chart below. Record your percentage on the graph on page 105.

_____ Total Score for Parts A, B, and C

_____ Percentage

Total Score	1	2	3	4	5	6	7	8	9	10	11	12	13	14	15	16	17
Percentage	6	12	18	24	29	35	41	47	53	59	65	71	76	82	88	94	100

Compare and Contrast

◆ Think about the celebrities, or famous people, in Unit Three. Pick two articles that tell about celebrities who are successful but who are not liked by everybody. Use information from the articles to fill in this chart.

Celebrity's Name		
In what way is the celebrity successful?		
Why do some people dislike the celebrity?		
How does the celebrity respond to being disliked?		

Glossary

A

abandoning   leaving something or someone behind   p. 57

abusive   harmful to other people   p. 78

accent   the way people say words that shows where they are from   p. 5

amateur   a person who does something for fun, not to earn money   p. 36

appealing   likeable or pleasing   p. 46

artificial   not real or not natural   p. 47

attitude   a way of thinking, acting, or feeling about something   p. 24

B

believable   accepted as true or real   p. 81

bleak   not good or without hope   p. 24

C

cartoonists   people who create cartoons   p. 88

certificate   a paper which lists the facts about something   p. 56

classical   a kind of music that began in the 1700s, such as music written by Mozart   p. 4

condiments   something eaten with food to make the food taste better   p. 14

conservative against change or not liking new ideas p. 88

consultant someone whose job is to give helpful information p. 81

content not wanting anything more than what you already have p. 17

cynical believing that most people do things for themselves, not for others p. 88

G

glamorous full of beauty and excitement p. 68

glory the special attention that people give to someone who they think is great p. 26

gossip talk about the personal business of other people, often in a mean way p. 70

H

humble not thinking or acting like you are more important than others p. 24

I

issue to give p. 58

J

judo a sport like wrestling, in which the athletes try to tip each other over p. 80

L

luxury a state of being very comfortable and having everything you want p. 56

M

miserable   very unhappy or not comfortable   p. 46

moral   concerned with being good and doing the right thing   p. 89

P

par   in golf, a set number of strokes a good player would take to finish a hole or a course   p. 38

passion   a strong liking for something   p. 7

petrified   not able to move because of fear   p. 15

pianist   a person who plays the piano   p. 4

pressure   a heavy feeling caused by worry   p. 15

priority   something that's important or that needs to come first   p. 59

privacy   freedom from being watched or bothered by other people   p. 71

professional   doing something in order to earn money and make a living   p. 36

Q

qualify   to be considered good enough   p. 36

R

reaction   something that a person does or feels because of something that has happened   p. 4

recovery   a return to health after being sick or hurt   p. 80

reputation   the way people think about someone because of what has happened in the past   p. 48

romantic   someone who enjoys thoughts and feelings of love   p. 47

S

suburbs   towns that are close to a city but aren't as busy as the city   p. 88

suffer   to feel pain or go through hard times   p. 14

T

tournament   a group of contests or games   p. 36

trials   difficult tests of a person's inner strength   p. 68

U

ultimate   greatest   p. 69

W

wide receiver   a football player who lines up at the end of a row of players and runs to catch the ball   p. 24

My Personal Dictionary

_____

_____

_____

_____

_____

_____

_____

_____

_____

_____

_____

_____

_____

_____

My Personal Dictionary

Writing Checklist

1. I followed the directions for writing.

2. My writing shows that I read and understood the article.

3. I capitalized the names of people.

4. I capitalized the proper names of places and things.

5. I read my writing aloud and listened for missing words.

6. I used a dictionary to check words that don't look right.

◆ Use the chart below to check off the things on the list that you have done.

✓ Checklist Numbers	Lesson Numbers								
	1	2	3	4	5	6	7	8	9
1.									
2.									
3.									
4.									
5.									
6.									

Progress Check

You can take charge of your own progress. The Comprehension and Critical Thinking Progress Graph on the next page can help you. Use it to keep track of how you are doing as you work through the lessons in this book. Check the graph often with your teacher. What types of skills cause you trouble? Talk with your teacher about ways to work on these.

A sample Comprehension and Critical Thinking Progress Graph is shown below. The first three lessons have been filled in to show you how to use the graph.

Sample Comprehension and Critical Thinking Progress Graph

◆ **Directions:** Write your percentage score for each lesson in the box under the number of the lesson. Then put a small X on the line. The X goes above the number of the lesson and across from the score you earned. Chart your progress by drawing a line to connect the Xs.

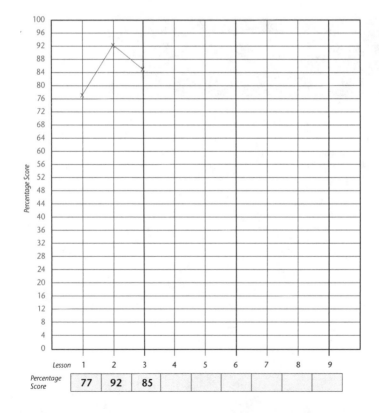

Lesson	1	2	3	4	5	6	7	8	9
Percentage Score	77	92	85						

Comprehension and Critical Thinking Progress Graph

◆ **Directions:** Write your percentage score for each lesson in the box
under the number of the lesson. Then put a small X on the line. The
X goes above the number of the lesson and across from the score you
earned. Chart your progress by drawing a line to connect the Xs.

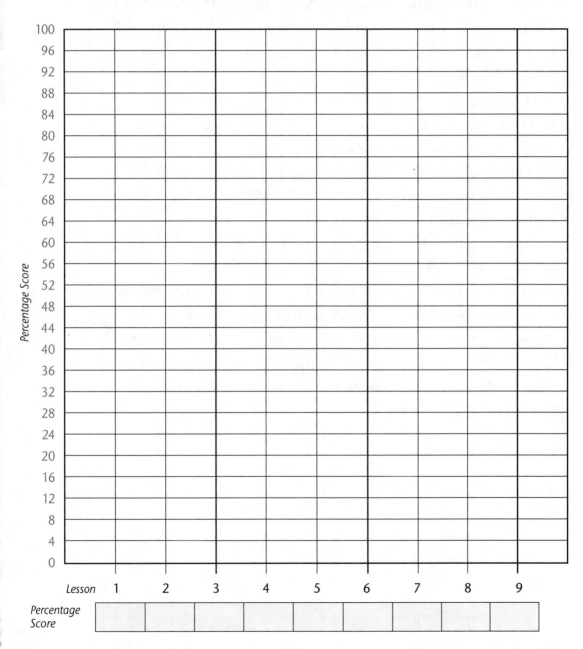

Photo Credits

Cover Al Bello/Getty Images, (inset)Robert Galbraith/Reuters/
CORBIS; 1 (t)Ted Aljibe/Getty Images, (c)CARDINALE STEPHANE/
CORBIS SYGMA, (b)Andy Lyons/Getty Images; 2 Marcus Brandt/
Getty Images; 7 Ted Aljibe/Getty Images; 12 Vince Bucci/Getty
Images; 17 CARDINALE STEPHANE/CORBIS SYGMA;
22 Ezra Shaw/Getty Images; 27 Andy Lyons/Getty Images;
33 (t)Yun Jai-hyoung/AP/Wide World Photos, (c)Clive Coote/
Miramax Films/Bureau L.A. Collections/CORBIS, (b)Kevin Winter/
Getty Images; 34 Robert Galbraith/Reuters/CORBIS;
39 Yun Jai-hyoung/AP/Wide World Photos; 43 Pat Lewis; 44 Reuters/
CORBIS; 49 Clive Coote/Miramax Films/Bureau L.A. Collections/
CORBIS; 54 Carlo Allegri/Getty Images; 59 Kevin Winter/Getty
Images; 65 (t)Tore Bergsaker/Sygma/CORBIS, (c)Courtesy
Walter P. Dean for the United States Association of Blind Athletes,
(b)Gail Burton/AP/Wide World Photos; 66 Dave Hogan/Getty Images;
71 Tore Bergsaker/Sygma/CORBIS; 76 Craig Schwartz; 81 Courtesy
Walter P. Dean for the United States Association of Blind Athletes;
86 Lucy Nicholson/AP/Wide World Photos; 91 Gail Burton/AP/
Wide World Photos.